P9-CRW-626

AFRICAN AMERICAN ANSWER BOOK

BIOGRAPHY

AFRICAN AMERICAN ANSWER BOOK

BIOGRAPHY

325 QUESTIONS

R. S. Rennert

Chelsea House Publishers
Philadelphia

CHELSEA HOUSE PUBLISHERS

EDITORIAL DIRECTOR Richard Rennert
EXECUTIVE MANAGING EDITOR Karyn Gullen Browne
COPY CHIEF Robin James
PICTURE EDITOR Adrian G. Allen
ART DIRECTOR Robert Mitchell
MANUFACTURING DIRECTOR Gerald Levine
ASSISTANT ART DIRECTOR Joan Ferrigno

AFRICAN AMERICAN ANSWER BOOK

SERIES ORIGINATOR AND ADVISER Ken Butkus
ASSISTANT EDITOR Annie McDonnell
DESIGNER John Infantino
PICTURE RESEARCHER Sandy Jones

5   7   9   8   6

Library of Congress Cataloging-in-Publication Data
Rennert, Richard Scott, 1956-
African American answer book, biography /R.S. Rennert.

   p. cm.
Includes index.
ISBN 0-7910-3203-5
      0-7910-3204-3 (pbk.)
1. Afro-Americans—Biography—Miscellanea—
Juvenile literature. [1. Afro-Americans—Biography—
Miscellanea. 2. Questions and answers.] I. W. E. B.
Du Bois Institute for Afro-American Research. II. Title.
E185.96.R45 1995   94-30201
920'.009296073—dc20   CIP
                                            AC

PICTURE CREDITS

AP/Wide World Photos: p. 47; Beinecke Rare Book
and Manuscript Library, Yale University: p. 10; The
Bettmann Archive: pp. 15, 30, 50; Ohio Historical
Society: p. 22; UPI/Bettmann: pp. 25, 34, 39, 44.

CONTENTS

INTRODUCTION

In creating the BLACK AMERICANS OF ACHIEVEMENT series for Chelsea House Publishers, I was fortunate enough to work closely with Nathan Irvin Huggins, one of America's leading scholars in the field of black studies and director of the W. E. B. Du Bois Institute for Afro-American Research at Harvard University. His innumerable contributions to the books have not only helped to make BLACK AMERICANS OF ACHIEVEMENT an award-winning series, but his expressed commitment to inform readers about the rich heritage and accomplishments of African Americans has encouraged Chelsea House to draw from his work and develop the 325 questions that make up this *African American Answer Book.*

Each of these briskly challenging questions has been designed to stimulate thought and discussion about African American history. The answers highlight either the leading figures of black America or focus on previously unsung yet equally inspiring African American heroes, their achievements, and their legacies.

You can use these questions to test your own knowledge or to stump your friends. Either way, you will find that this *African American Answer Book*—like its companion volumes—is bound to educate as well as entertain.

—**R. S. R.**

QUESTIONS

1. Henry Aaron finished his baseball career with what team?

    a - *Milwaukee Brewers*
    b - *Atlanta Braves*
    c - *Milwaukee Braves*

2. Henry Aaron ended his baseball career as the all-time home run king. How many home runs did he hit?

    a - *755*
    b - *765*
    c - *777*

3. What nickname was given to Henry Aaron due to his lightning quick home run swing?

    a - *Hammerin' Hank*
    b - *Slammin' Hank*
    c - *Blastin' Hank*

4. What year did Henry Aaron win his first National League batting title?

    a - *1951*
    b - *1953*
    c - *1956*

5. (True or False) Henry Aaron led the New York Yankees to a World Series victory in 1957.

6. What boxer gave Muhammad Ali his first professional loss?

    a - *Leon Spinks*
    b - *Joe Frazier*
    c - *Sonny Liston*

7. Who coined Ali's slogan "Float like a butterfly, sting like a bee"?

    a - *Drew "Bundini" Brown*
    b - *Angelo Dundee*
    c - *Howard Cosell*

8. What boxer did Muhammad Ali defeat to earn the heavyweight championship title?

    a - *George Foreman*
    b - *Mike Tyson*
    c - *Jack Johnson*

9. (True or False) Muhammad Ali was the first person to win the world heavyweight title three times.

10. What did Muhammad Ali do with the gold medal for boxing he won at the 1960 Olympics?

    a - *Sold it and donated the proceeds to the Nation of Islam*
    b - *Threw it in the Ohio River to protest America's racism*
    c - *Wore it in a boxing match*

11. (True or False) Richard Allen was born into slavery on a Philadelphia estate in 1760.

12. Richard Allen spearheaded the fight against racial discrimination through his church ministry. What was the name of his church?

    a - *Ebenezer Baptist Church*
    b - *First Colored Presbyterian Church*
    c - *African Methodist Episcopal Church*

13. What was the name of the first national black convention that was organized by Richard Allen in 1830?

    a - *American Society of Free Persons of Colour*
    b - *Niagara Movement*
    c - *Southern Christian Leadership Conference*

14. Why did Richard Allen storm out of St. George's Methodist Church during a morning service in 1787?

    a - *The minister used a racial slur in his sermon*
    b - *He disagreed with the church's theology*
    c - *The church had a discriminatory seating policy*

15. (True or False) Richard Allen was the first bishop of what is now the oldest black established church in the United States?

16. In what city was Marian Anderson born?

    a - *Philadelphia*
    b - *Chicago*
    c - *Boston*

17. What was Marian Anderson sometimes called?

    a - *"Voice of the American Soul"*
    b - *"Queen of Soul"*
    c - *"Voice of Pearls"*

18. (True or False) In 1955, Marian Anderson became only the third black singer to perform with the Metropolitan Opera.

19. In 1958, President Dwight Eisenhower appointed Marian Anderson:

    a - *U.S. delegate to the United Nations*
    b - *To the U.S. Senate*
    c - *Member of the Committee for the National Arts Foundation*

20. The Daughters of the Revolution (DAR) did not allow Marian Anderson to perform at Constitution Hall. What happened after this incident?

    a - *Marian Anderson sued for discrimination*
    b - *Eleanor Roosevelt publicly announced her resignation from the DAR*
    c - *Marian Anderson forced her way into Constitution Hall in order to perform*

21. Where was Louis Armstrong born?

    a - *Chicago*
    b - *New York City*
    c - *New Orleans*

22. What song recorded by Louis Armstrong became the nation's number one record in 1964?

    a - *"One O'Clock Jump"*
    b - *"Fly Me to the Moon"*
    c - *"Hello Dolly"*

An international sensation, Josephine Baker made herself into "a complete artist, the perfect master of her tools," and a hugely successful nightclub performer and film star.

23. What was Louis Armstrong's nickname?

    a - *Satchmo*
    b - *Duke*
    c - *Dizzy*

24. What type of music did Louis Armstrong revolutionize and help establish as the nation's first highly popular black art form?

    a - *Jazz*
    b - *Bebop*
    c - *Dixie*

25. What was the name of the famous jazz band Louis Armstrong joined in Chicago in 1922?

    a - *Deans of Swing*
    b - *King Oliver's Creole Jazz Band*
    c - *Barons of Rhythm*

26. Arthur Ashe remains the only African American to gain recognition for what accomplishment?

    a - *Ranked in the top 15 of men's tennis*
    b - *Ranked number one in men's tennis*
    c - *Sportsman of the Year*

27. In 1975, Arthur Ashe won the Wimbledon men's singles title, defeating who in the final match?

    a - *Bjorn Borg*
    b - *Rod Laver*
    c - *Jimmy Connors*

28. In 1979, what forced Arthur Ashe to retire from professional tennis?

    a - *HIV infection*
    b - *Leg injuries*
    c - *Heart attack*

29. In 1968, Arthur Ashe became the first African American to win what major tennis tournament?

    a - *Australian Open*
    b - *Wimbledon*
    c - *U.S. Open*

30. In 1992, what prestigious award did Arthur Ashe receive, making him the first person to attain this honor after retiring from a professional sport?

    a - *Sportsman of the Year*
    b - *Spingarn Medal*
    c - *Associated Press's Athlete of the Decade*

31. What was the name of Josephine Baker's most famous dance?

    a - *The Twist*
    b - *The Charleston*
    c - *The Ballet*

32. What was significant about Josephine Baker's performance at Carnegie Hall?

  a - *Benefit performance for the civil rights movement*
  b - *Lifetime achievement celebration*
  c - *Her final performance*

33. Who recruited Josephine Baker as a "secret agent" during World War II?

  a - *French Military Intelligence*
  b - *CIA*
  c - *U.S. Secret Service*

34. Josephine Baker was awarded which prestigious medals?

  a - *Spingarn Medal/NAACP Image Award*
  b - *Rosette of the Resistance/Legion of Honor*
  c - *Nobel Peace Prize/Spingarn Medal*

35. What music hall performance turned Josephine Baker into a living legend?

  a - *Folies-Bergère*
  b - *Moulin Rouge*
  c - *Preservation Hall*

36. What was James Baldwin's book, *Go Tell It on the Mountain* about?

  a - *A young minister in Harlem*
  b - *An interracial marriage*
  c - *An aspiring writer*

37. James Baldwin was regarded as a writer who argued for:

  a - *Accommodationism*
  b - *Racial understanding*
  c - *Black militancy*

38. Who did Baldwin advise during the Birmingham crisis?

  a - *Martin Luther King, Jr.*
  b - *Malcolm X*
  c - *Robert F. Kennedy*

39. James Baldwin wrote about the civil rights movement and the relationship between blacks and whites in which of the following books?

    a - *Notes of a Native Son; The Fire Next Time*
    b - *If He Hollers Let Him Go; Lonely Crusade*
    c - *The Weary Blues; Not Without Laughter*

40. (True or False) James Baldwin was one of the first American writers to treat homosexuality straightforwardly and respectfully in his work *Giovanni's Room*.

41. (True or False) Benjamin Banneker published the first scientific work by an African American.

42. What did Benjamin Banneker publish that was extremely useful for farmers?

    a - *Atlas*
    b - *Almanac*
    c - *Crop rotation guide*

43. Benjamin Banneker assisted in the survey of what major U.S. city?

    a - *Chicago*
    b - *New York*
    c - *Washington, D.C.*

44. In 1753, what did Benjamin Banneker build?

    a - *The first telescope in the American colonies*
    b - *The first wooden clock in the American colonies*
    c - *The first steel structure in the American colonies*

45. Benjamin Banneker convinced what U.S. president that African Americans were intelligent and deserved to be free?

    a - *Thomas Jefferson*
    b - *Andrew Jackson*
    c - *Abraham Lincoln*

46. What was Amiri Baraka's given name?

    a - *LeRoi Jones*
    b - *Count Basie*
    c - *Duke Ellington*

47. In 1963, Amiri Baraka published a study of African American music entitled:

   a - *All That Jazz*
   b - *Blues People*
   c - *Tales of Black Music*

48. Amiri Baraka's *Dutchman, The Baptism, The Slave,* and *The Toilet* were:

   a - *Novels*
   b - *Plays*
   c - *Collections of poetry*

49. Amiri Baraka helped to organize:

   a - *Congressional Black Congress*
   b - *Congress of Racial Equality*
   c - *Congress of Afrikan Peoples*

50. Amiri Baraka founded the Black Arts Repertory Theater/School, which is located in what city?

   a - *Harlem (New York City)*
   b - *Chicago*
   c - *Philadelphia*

51. (True or False) Count Basie started his career by playing music in theaters to accompany silent movies.

52. What song has become Count Basie's theme song and was later recorded by many different music groups?

   a - *"One O'Clock Jump"*
   b - *"Rock Around the Clock"*
   c - *"Maple Leaf Rag"*

53. What famous female vocalist toured with "The Count Basie Orchestra"?

   a - *Marian Anderson*
   b - *Mahalia Jackson*
   c - *Billie Holiday*

54. What recording, performed by Count Basie and sung by Frank Sinatra, was played on the moon by U.S. astronauts on July 20, 1969?

   a - *"Moon River"*
   b - *"Blue Moon"*
   c - *"Fly Me to the Moon"*

One of America's preeminent jazz pianists and bandleaders for more than half a century, William "Count" Basie specialized in the Kansas City sound—a swinging, bluesy jazz—and popularized it around the world.

55. Count Basie won his first Grammy Award in 1963 for instrumental arrangement of what song?

    a - *"Every Day I Have the Blues"*
    b - *"I Can't Stop Loving You"*
    c - *"Hello Dolly"*

56. (True or False) Romare Bearden is best known for his stunning collages.

57. To support himself as an artist, Romare Bearden worked as a:

    a - *Social worker*
    b - *Teacher*
    c - *Insurance salesman*

58. In 1987, Romare Bearden was awarded the highly prestigious:

    a - *Spingarn Medal*
    b - *National Medal of Arts*
    c - *Pulitzer Prize*

59. In addition to being a respected artist, Romare Bearden was:

    a - *A singer*
    b - *A distinguished art historian*
    c - *A part-time jazz musician*

60. (True or False) Playwright August Wilson described Bearden's art as "black life presented on its own terms, on a grand and epic scale, with all its richness and fullness."

61. What was the name of the route discovered by James Beckwourth?

    a - *Sierra Madre Pass*
    b - *Continental Divide*
    c - *Beckwourth Pass*

62. (True or False) James Beckwourth was one of America's first black frontiersmen, in the company of such celebrated frontiersmen of that time as Jedediah Smith, Jim Bridger, and James Clyman.

63. James Beckwourth led the first wagon train through the:

    a - *Appalachian Mountains*
    b - *Sierra Nevada*
    c - *Rocky Mountains*

64. James Beckwourth started a trading post that led to what settlement?

    a - *Sacramento, California*
    b - *Pueblo, Colorado*
    c - *Taos, New Mexico*

65. James Beckwourth became a part of what Native American tribe?

    a - *The Crow*
    b - *The Comanche*
    c - *The Cherokee*

66. Mary McLeod Bethune practiced the philosophy of what prominent educator?

    a - *Rufus Clement*
    b - *Booker T. Washington*
    c - *Benjamin Mays*

67. Starting with $1.50 in cash, what college did Mary McLeod Bethune found?

    a - *Bethune-Cookman College*
    b - *Mary McLeod Bethune College*
    c - *Tuskegee Institute*

68. Mary McLeod Bethune joined forces with other prominent African Americans who were appointed to administrative positions by Franklin Roosevelt. This group of federal officials was referred to as the nation's:

    a - *Black Cabinet*
    b - *Black Council*
    c - *Black Advisors*

69. Mary McLeod Bethune was the founder and president of what national association?

    a - *National Association of Colored Women*
    b - *National Council of Negro Women*
    c - *National Association of Teachers in Colored Schools*

70. In 1936, Mary McLeod Bethune became the first black woman to head what federal agency created to combat unemployment among young African Americans?

    a - *Division of Negro Affairs, National Youth Administration*
    b - *Department of Health and Human Services*
    c - *Department of Housing and Urban Development*

71. Ralph Bunche was a recognized expert in:

    a - *African American history*
    b - *Race relations*
    c - *Lobbying legislators*

72. (True or False) In 1950, Ralph Bunche became the first African American to receive a Nobel Prize.

73. Ralph Bunche was a high-ranking official in:

    a - *The U.S. State Department*
    b - *The United Nations*
    c - *Both a & b*

74. Bunche studied in and traveled extensively through:

    a - *The Middle East*
    b - *Southeast Asia*
    c - *Africa*

75. Ralph Bunche earned the Nobel Peace Prize for his work in:

    a - *Helping to end colonialism and establish independent African nations*
    b - *Mediating the Arab-Israeli conflict*
    c - *Working against apartheid in South Africa*

76. (True or False) George Washington Carver's experiments with crop rotation proved that certain crops, such as peanuts and sweet potatoes, returned nutrients to the soil.

77. Approximately how many different products did George Washington Carver develop from peanuts?

    a - *50*
    b - *150*
    c - *325*

78. What famous inventor offered George Washington Carver a job?

    a - *Henry Ford*
    b - *Thomas Edison*
    c - *Alexander Graham Bell*

79. In what year was George Washington Carver born?

    a - *1834*
    b - *1864*
    c - *1894*

80. Who was the principal at Tuskegee Institute who recruited and hired George Washington Carver?

    a - *Calvin H. Washington*
    b - *Robert Russa Moton*
    c - *Booker T. Washington*

81. Charles Chesnutt was America's first published:

    a - *Black poet*
    b - *Black novelist*
    c - *Black playwright*

82. Charles Chesnutt's first published work was called *Uncle Peter's House*. He sold this to the *Cleveland News and Herald* for how much?

    a - *$5.00*
    b - *$10.00*
    c - *$500.00*

83. What was the name of Charles Chesnutt's first novel?

    a - *The House Behind the Cedars*
    b - *Native Son*
    c - *Uncle Tom's Cabin*

84. One of Charles Chesnutt's most important themes was:

    a - *The struggle for freedom in Africa*
    b - *The fate of mixed-bloods in a racist society*
    c - *A call for militant nationalism*

85. (True or False) In 1928, the NAACP gave Charles Chesnutt the Spingarn Medal for the "highest or noblest achievement by an American Negro."

86. Where was Bill Cosby born and raised?

    a - *Detroit*
    b - *New York City*
    c - *Philadelphia*

87. (True or False) Bill Cosby dropped out of school in the 11th grade to join the navy.

88. What character did Bill Cosby portray on "The Cosby Show"?

    a - *Dr. Cliff Huxtable*
    b - *Alexander Scott*
    c - *Chet Kincaid*

89. What was the name of Bill Cosby's first best-selling book?

    a - *Fatherhood*
    b - *The World According to Me*
    c - *The Bill Cosby Story*

90. Bill Cosby, the first black in a nontraditional role, won an Emmy Award for best actor in 1966 for his performance in what television series?

    a - *"The Mod Squad"*
    b - *"I Spy"*
    c - *"Cos"*

91. (True or False) Paul Cuffe wanted to establish a black homeland in the Caribbean.

92. Paul Cuffe owned what kind of company?

    a - *Shipbuilding and shipping*
    b - *Hair care products*
    c - *Publishing*

93. Paul Cuffe established a lucrative trade partnership with what African country?

    a - *Zimbabwe*
    b - *Uganda*
    c - *Sierra Leone*

94. What black nationalist leader promoted a "Back to Africa" movement that was similar in concept to Paul Cuffe's?

    a - *Marcus Garvey*
    b - *Malcolm X*
    c - *W. E. B. Du Bois*

95. What did Paul Cuffe do to protest the lack of suffrage for blacks in Massachusetts?

    a - *Picketed the polling places*
    b - *Refused to pay taxes*
    c - *Founded a civil rights organization*

96. Frederick Douglass was ambassador to:

    a - *Liberia*
    b - *Haiti*
    c - *Panama*

97. What was the name of the influential antislavery newspaper published by Frederick Douglass?

    a - *The North Star*
    b - *The Crusader*
    c - *The Defender*

98. During the Civil War, Frederick Douglass served as an adviser to what U.S. president?

    a - *Ulysses S. Grant*
    b - *Thomas Jefferson*
    c - *Abraham Lincoln*

99. (True or False) Frederick Douglass was a Republican who held political positions in the administrations of Lincoln, Grant, Hayes, and Garfield?

100. Frederick Douglass provided a powerful voice for human rights and fought for the ratification of what amendment that guaranteed all citizens the right to vote, regardless of their race?

> **a** - *Thirteenth Amendment*
> **b** - *Fourteenth Amendment*
> **c** - *Fifteenth Amendment*

101. Charles Drew spearheaded the world's first:

> **a** - *Organ donor program*
> **b** - *Heart transplant*
> **c** - *Blood bank program*

102. What organization did Charles Drew resign from in response to the U.S. War Department's order to segregate "white" and "black" blood?

> **a** - *United Way*
> **b** - *U.S. Navy*
> **c** - *American Red Cross*

103. Charles Drew became the first African American to obtain what degree?

> **a** - *Doctor of Science in Mathematics*
> **b** - *Doctor of Science in Medicine*
> **c** - *Doctor of Psychiatry*

104. What is the name of the famous black college in Washington, D.C., where Charles Drew taught medicine?

> **a** - *Meharry Medical College*
> **b** - *Howard University*
> **c** - *Morehouse College*

105. (True or False) Charles Drew, who taught more than half of the black surgeons certified during the 1940s, led the campaign to integrate the American Medical Association.

106. (True or False) In 1905, W. E. B. Du Bois founded the Niagara Movement, a protest organization that included many northern black intellectuals.

Paul Laurence Dunbar, the first internationally known African American poet and novelist, was, according to one critic, "the first man of his color to study his race objectively. . . . to represent it humorously, yet tenderly, and above all . . . faithfully."

107. W. E. B. Du Bois cofounded what national organization?

    a - *National Association for the Advancement of Colored People*
    b - *Congress of Racial Equality*
    c - *United Negro College Fund*

108. What is the name of the newsletter originally edited by W. E. B. Du Bois?

    a - *The Crisis*
    b - *Defender*
    c - *New Crusader*

109. W. E. B. Du Bois was the first African American to receive a Ph.D. from what prestigious university?

    a - *Yale*
    b - *Harvard*
    c - *University of Pennsylvania*

110. In 1961, W. E. B. Du Bois renounced his U.S. citizenship and became a citizen of what country?

    a - *South Africa*
    b - *Ghana*
    c - *Canada*

111. Paul Laurence Dunbar started writing poems at what age?

    a - *6*
    b - *12*
    c - *30*

112. (True or False) Paul Laurence Dunbar was born into freedom in Dayton, Ohio.

113. (True or False) Though he wrote in the romantic style of Keats and Shelley, Dunbar celebrated the nobility of ordinary people and captured the rhythms of black speech.

114. What anthology of poems written by Paul Laurence Dunbar received worldwide acclaim?

    a - *Lyrics of Lowly Life*
    b - *The Bean Eaters*
    c - *The Weary Blues*

115. Who helped promote Paul Laurence Dunbar's poetry and became his good friends?

    a - *Charles Chesnutt and Booker T. Washington*
    b - *Ida Wells-Barnett and Frederick Douglass*
    c - *Orville and Wilbur Wright*

116. What type of dance rhythms and movements did Katherine Dunham introduce to the American stage?

    a - *African and Caribbean*
    b - *Middle Eastern*
    c - *Far Eastern*

117. In 1979, Katherine Dunham received what prestigious award?

    a - *Tony Award*
    b - *Albert Schweitzer Music Award*
    c - *Academy Award*

118. Besides being a dancer, Katherine Dunham was also a trained:

  a - *Actress*
  b - *Anthropologist*
  c - *Classical pianist*

119. In 1963, Katherine Dunham became the first African American choreographer to work at what New York City theater?

  a - *Metropolitan Opera House*
  b - *Windsor Theater*
  c - *Cotton Club*

120. In 1940, what was the name of the dance show performed on Broadway that propelled Katherine Dunham to stardom?

  a - *Carnival of Rhythm*
  b - *Tropics and Le Jazz Hot: From Haiti to Harlem*
  c - *Negro Rhapsody*

121. What form of music did Duke Ellington elevate into a serious art form?

  a - *Ragtime*
  b - *Jazz*
  c - *Blues*

122. In 1927, Duke Ellington's band began a successful engagement at what celebrated Harlem club?

  a - *Folies-Bergère*
  b - *The Cotton Club*
  c - *The Apollo*

123. What was Duke Ellington's real name?

  a - *Edward Kennedy Ellington*
  b - *John Hodges Ellington*
  c - *Charlie Parker*

124. Approximately how many musical compositions did Duke Ellington write?

  a - *500*
  b - *1,000*
  c - *2,000*

Hailed by critics as the "first pioneer of the Negro dance," Katherine Dunham realized worldwide success with her captivating choreography and trained a generation of black dancers, including Arthur Mitchell and Eartha Kitt.

125. In 1941, what jazz piece performed by Duke Ellington and His Orchestra became an instant hit?

    a - *"Maple Leaf Rag"*
    b - *"Take the 'A' Train"*
    c - *"Creole Rhapsody"*

126. Ralph Ellison turned to writing after his career in what field was unsuccessful?

    a - *Acting*
    b - *Politics*
    c - *Music*

127. What famous African American encouraged Ralph Ellison's efforts to become a writer?

    a - *Alex Haley*
    b - *Richard Wright*
    c - *James Baldwin*

128. In 1953, Ralph Ellison became the first African American to receive the National Book Award. For what book was he honored?

> **a** - *Invisible Man*
> **b** - *Go Tell It on the Mountain*
> **c** - *Native Son*

129. (True or False) Ellison was an important part of the militant black nationalist movement, writing about African roots.

130. In Ralph Ellison's book *Shadow and Act,* he discussed:

> **a** - *How deeply American culture has been influenced by the black experience*
> **b** - *How African Americans are made to feel invisible*
> **c** - *His appreciation of African American art and music*

131. (True or False) James Farmer organized the first nonviolent protest of the civil rights movement.

132. What organization was formed by James Farmer in 1942?

> **a** - *National Urban Coalition*
> **b** - *Congress of Racial Equality*
> **c** - *Student Nonviolent Coordinating Committee*

133. Which of the following civil rights protests were organized by James Farmer?

> **a** - *Montgomery bus boycott; Poor Peoples' Campaign*
> **b** - *Selma March; March on Washington*
> **c** - *Sit-in Movement; Freedom Rides*

134. Who defeated James Farmer in his run for a Congressional seat?

> **a** - *Shirley Chisholm*
> **b** - *Adam Clayton Powell, Jr.*
> **c** - *Barbara Jordan*

135. What did the Freedom Riders seek to accomplish?

> **a** - *To stop the Ku Klux Klan*
> **b** - *To integrate interstate travel and bus stations*
> **c** - *To support the Montgomery bus boycott*

136. What is Ella Fitzgerald often called?

    a - *"Queen of Soul"*
    b - *"Queen of the Blues"*
    c - *"First Lady of Song"*

137. What company's popular commercial featured a tape recording of Ella Fitzgerald's voice shattering a glass?

    a - *Memorex*
    b - *3M*
    c - *Sony*

138. Which song was made popular by Ella Fitzgerald?

    a - *"Georgia on My Mind"*
    b - *"Love You Madly"*
    c - *"You Are the Sunshine of My Life"*

139. What hit song made Ella Fitzgerald a national celebrity at the age of 20?

    a - *"A Tisket, a Tasket"*
    b - *"Poem of Love"*
    c - *"I'm Your Baby Tonight"*

140. What orchestra did Ella Fitzgerald sing with and eventually become the leader of?

    a - *Electric Light Orchestra*
    b - *Count Basie Orchestra*
    c - *Chick Webb Orchestra*

141. Marcus Garvey emerged after World War I as a champion of black rights and the charismatic leader of what movement?

    a - *Black Muslim movement*
    b - *Back to Africa movement*
    c - *Civil rights movement*

142. What was Marcus Garvey's nickname?

    a - *Black Moses*
    b - *Black Disciple*
    c - *Black Messiah*

143. What organization formed by Marcus Garvey promoted racial pride and self-improvement?

  a - *Congress of Racial Equality*
  b - *Nation of Islam*
  c - *Universal Negro Improvement Association*

144. What was the name of Marcus Garvey's shipping company that was owned and operated entirely by blacks?

  a - *Traveller Shipping Company*
  b - *Black Star Line*
  c - *Booker T. Washington & Company*

145. What great African American educator influenced Marcus Garvey's commitment to self-improvement?

  a - *W. E. B. Du Bois*
  b - *Booker T. Washington*
  c - *Mary McLeod Bethune*

146. (True or False) Althea Gibson became the first African American to compete in the U.S. Lawn Tennis Association Tournaments.

147. What major tournament did Althea Gibson win in 1956?

  a - *U.S. Open*
  b - *French Championship*
  c - *Wimbledon*

148. (True or False) Althea Gibson was born to a middle-class black family in South Carolina.

149. What consecutive years did Althea Gibson win the Wimbledon Tennis Singles Championship?

  a - *1950, 1951*
  b - *1957, 1958*
  c - *1960, 1961*

150. After retiring from professional tennis, Althea Gibson launched a new professional sports career in:

    a - *Golf*
    b - *Track and field*
    c - *Basketball*

151. (True or False) Matthew Henson was the first man to reach the North Pole.

152. Matthew Henson learned the language and skills of what Indian tribe?

    a - *Crow*
    b - *Mohawk*
    c - *Inuit*

153. In what year did Matthew Henson reach the top of the North Pole?

    a - *1909*
    b - *1919*
    c - *1929*

154. Approximately how many years did it take Matthew Henson and Robert Peary to reach the top of the North Pole?

    a - *10*
    b - *18*
    c - *30*

155. Matthew Henson also explored:

    a - *Africa*
    b - *China*
    c - *Nicaragua*

156. What detective story written by Chester Himes became a motion picture?

    a - *Black Betty*
    b - *Cotton Comes to Harlem*
    c - *Their Eyes Were Watching God*

157. At the age of 19, where did Chester Himes write the short stories that were published in several prominent magazines?

    a - *Harvard University*
    b - *Prison*
    c - *Cleveland ghetto*

Beloved by fans as "Lady Day," Billie Holiday used the heartbreak she had experienced in life to infuse her sophisticated vocals with raw emotional honesty.

158. Whom did Chester Himes satirize in one of his famous detective novels?

    a - *Marcus Garvey*
    b - *Booker T. Washington*
    c - *Josephine Baker*

159. (True or False) Chester Himes started as a protest writer but changed to detective fiction because he "knew the life of an American black needed another image than just the victim of racism."

160. What book is an autobiography of Chester Himes's life?

    a - *Cotton Comes to Harlem*
    b - *If He Hollers Let Him Go*
    c - *The Quality of Hurt*

161. Billie Holiday became one of the world's most distinctive:

    a - *Jazz singers*
    b - *Gospel singers*
    c - *Opera singers*

162. Billie Holiday's autobiography was called:

    a - *Lady Sings the Blues*
    b - *I Know Why the Caged Bird Sings*
    c - *Good Morning, Blues*

163. What led to the downfall of Billie Holiday's brilliant singing career?

    a - *Drug abuse*
    b - *Vocal chord damage*
    c - *Car accident*

164. Billie Holiday performed with what great bandleader?

    a - *Scott Joplin*
    b - *Count Basie*
    c - *Dizzy Gillespie*

165. In 1939, what recording by Billie Holiday became a powerful plea for black civil rights?

    a - *"Gloomy Sunday"*
    b - *"Strange Fruit"*
    c - *"Trav'lin All Alone"*

166. Langston Hughes is best remembered as:

    a - *The poet of the black community*
    b - *The poet laureate of Harlem*
    c - *The pioneer of African American journalism*

167. (True or False) Langston Hughes earned a reputation as a "literary rebel" due to the strong social overtones in his work.

168. This poem was *not* written by Langston Hughes:

    a - *"The Weary Blues"*
    b - *"I, Too, Sing America"*
    c - *"Ode to Freedom"*

169. Langston Hughes introduced a new form of poetry that used elements of which musical style(s)?

   a - *Classical*
   b - *Jazz and blues*
   c - *Rock 'n' roll*

170. What was the main character's name in the famous series of short stories by Langston Hughes, in which a black Everyman reacts to racism with humor and quiet determination?

   a - *Bigger Thomas*
   b - *The Invisible Man*
   c - *Jess B. Semple*

171. What masterpiece of American literature was written by Zora Neale Hurston?

   a - *Go Tell It on the Mountain*
   b - *Their Eyes Were Watching God*
   c - *The Temple of My Familiar*

172. Why did Zora Neale Hurston travel through the South?

   a - *To study African American dance and song*
   b - *To protest racism*
   c - *To gather folklore*

173. What travel experiences had a profound impact on Zora Neale Hurston's writing?

   a - *Voodoo rituals in the Caribbean*
   b - *Black poverty in Louisiana*
   c - *France's acceptance of black artists*

174. In what movement was Zora Neale Hurston a leading figure?

   a - *Niagara movement*
   b - *Harlem Renaissance*
   c - *Women's rights movement*

175. (True or False) Toni Morrison found Zora Neale Hurston's unmarked grave in a segregated cemetery and placed a headstone there that read "A Genius of the South."

176. What organization was formed by Jesse Jackson?

  a - *UNCF*
  b - *Operation PUSH*
  c - *SCLC*

177. Who did Jesse Jackson impress with his work on Operation Breadbasket in Chicago?

  a - *Martin Luther King, Jr.*
  b - *Malcolm X*
  c - *Jimmy Carter*

178. Who did Jesse Jackson run against for the Democratic presidential nomination?

  a - *Ronald Reagan and George Bush*
  b - *Jimmy Carter and Walter Mondale*
  c - *Walter Mondale and Michael Dukakis*

179. (True or False) Jesse Jackson negotiated the release of nearly 300 hostages held by Iraq in 1990.

180. An inspirational speaker, Jesse Jackson is famous for saying:

  a - *"I have a dream."*
  b - *"Keep hope alive."*
  c - *"Black is beautiful."*

181. What type of poetry best describes James Weldon Johnson's "The Creation," "The Judgement Day," and "God's Trombones"?

  a - *Dramatic poetry*
  b - *Musical poetry*
  c - *Sermon poetry*

182. For what organization did James Weldon Johnson serve as executive secretary?

  a - *National Urban League*
  b - *National Association for the Advancement of Colored People*
  c - *Congress of Racial Equality*

183. What novel by James Weldon Johnson strongly influenced the writers of the Harlem Renaissance?

  a - *Up from Slavery*
  b - *The Autobiography of an Ex-Colored Man*
  c - *The Conjure Woman*

An impartial legislator who dealt with a wide range of issues including equal rights for minorities and women, Barbara Jordan gained national fame as an electrifying orator and a principled politician.

184. What is the name of the song written by James Weldon Johnson and his brother, J. Rosamond, which is regarded as the unofficial black national anthem?

      a - *"Amazing Grace"*
      b - *"Lift Every Voice and Sing"*
      c - *"We Shall Overcome"*

185. (True or False) James Weldon Johnson received diplomatic appointments to Venezuela and Nicaragua.

186. Scott Joplin played what instrument?

      a - *Trumpet*
      b - *Saxophone*
      c - *Piano*

187. What kind of music did composer Scott Joplin help to attain national prominence?

      a - *Jazz*
      b - *Ragtime*
      c - *Soul*

188. How much money did Scott Joplin earn for each piece of sheet music that was sold of his famous "Maple Leaf Rag"?

  a - *One cent*
  b - *Five cents*
  c - *Eight cents*

189. Scott Joplin was posthumously awarded:

  a - *A Pulitzer Prize*
  b - *A Grammy Award*
  c - *A Tony Lifetime Achievement Award*

190. What was the name of Scott Joplin's best known piece, which became the theme song for the Academy Award–winning movie *The Sting*?

  a - *"Maple Leaf Rag"*
  b - *"The Entertainer"*
  c - *"Ragtime"*

191. (True or False) In 1966, Barbara Jordan was elected to the Texas State Senate, becoming the first African American to sit in the Texas Senate since 1883.

192. Barbara Jordan became the South's first African American:

  a - *Governor*
  b - *Congresswoman*
  c - *Mayor*

193. Thurgood Marshall's victory in *Brown v. Board of Education of Topeka* inspired Jordan to:

  a - *Stage a sit-in at her university*
  b - *Become a lawyer*
  c - *Become a teacher at an integrated school*

194. Barbara Jordan's rousing keynote address at the Democratic National Convention helped elect what U.S. presidential candidate?

  a - *Bill Clinton*
  b - *Jimmy Carter*
  c - *Lyndon B. Johnson*

195. As a member of the 1974 House Judiciary Committee, Jordan earned national praise for doing what?

    a - *Calling for the impeachment of Richard Nixon*
    b - *Arguing that there was a conspiracy in the Kennedy assassination*
    c - *Approving the appointment of the first African American attorney general*

196. (True or False) Martin Luther King, Jr., was the first African American to win the Nobel Peace Prize.

197. In 1955, Martin Luther King, Jr., earned admiration for nonviolently leading:

    a - *The March on Washington*
    b - *The Montgomery bus boycott*
    c - *The Peace Pilgrimage*

198. In 1957, what organization was formed by Martin Luther King, Jr.?

    a - *National Association for the Advancement of Colored People*
    b - *Southern Christian Leadership Conference*
    c - *Student Nonviolent Coordinating Committee*

199. Where did Martin Luther King, Jr., utter the immortal words, "I still have a dream. It is a dream deeply rooted in the American dream"?

    a - *Selma*
    b - *The Birmingham jail*
    c - *The Lincoln Memorial*

200. Martin Luther King, Jr., played a part in organizing:

    a - *The March on Washington and the Selma march for voting rights*
    b - *The Chicago Freedom Movement and the Poor People's Campaign*
    c - *Both a & b*

201. Malcolm X electrified African Americans throughout the country by urging them to battle racial oppression with:

    a - *Nonviolent protest*
    b - *Political reform*
    c - *Militant action*

202. In 1949, while in prison, what religious movement did Malcolm X embrace?

  a - *Nation of Islam*
  b - *Baptist*
  c - *Catholic Liberation Theology*

203. Who cowrote *The Autobiography of Malcolm X*?

  a - *Langston Hughes*
  b - *Alex Haley*
  c - *James Baldwin*

204. What year was Malcolm X assassinated?

  a - *1959*
  b - *1963*
  c - *1965*

205. (True or False) Malcolm X founded a nonreligious civil rights group called the Organization of Afro-American Unity.

206. By the time Thurgood Marshall reached the age of 40, what nickname had he earned from the press?

  a - *Mr. Public Defender*
  b - *Mr. Civil Rights*
  c - *Mr. Labor Leader*

207. In 1954, what landmark Supreme Court case did Thurgood Marshall help orchestrate?

  a - *Brown v. Board of Education of Topeka*
  b - *Roe v. Wade*
  c - *Plessy v. Ferguson*

208. What U.S. president appointed Thurgood Marshall as the first African American justice on the U.S. Supreme Court?

  a - *John F. Kennedy*
  b - *Richard M. Nixon*
  c - *Lyndon B. Johnson*

209. (True or False) Thurgood Marshall was the first African American solicitor general, the nation's highest ranking courtroom advocate.

210. What was the significance of the *Brown v. Board of Education of Topeka* decision?

    a - *Determined that the "Separate but Equal" doctrine has no place in education*
    b - *Upheld the "Separate but Equal" doctrine*
    c - *Outlawed Jim Crow laws that had prevented blacks from voting for their local school boards of choice*

211. On January 28, 1986, what space shuttle exploded 73 seconds after lift-off, killing Ronald McNair and six of his colleagues?

    a - *Columbia*
    b - *Discovery*
    c - *Challenger*

212. (True or False) Ronald McNair was the first African American astronaut to journey into space.

213. As a member of the space shuttle team, what was Ronald McNair's responsibility?

    a - *Pilot*
    b - *Commander*
    c - *Mission science specialist*

214. (True or False) Ronald McNair earned a doctorate in physics from Harvard University.

215. (True or False) Ronald McNair played a part in developing new laser technology.

216. Toni Morrison's first novel, which explored the deep-seated effects of racism on concepts of beauty and self-esteem, was titled:

    a - *The Color Purple*
    b - *The Bluest Eye*
    c - *Tar Baby*

217. What was the name of Toni Morrison's Pulitzer Prize–winning novel about an escaped slave?

    a - *A Raisin in the Sun*
    b - *I Know Why the Caged Bird Sings*
    c - *Beloved*

218. (True or False) Toni Morrison was the first African American to win the Nobel Prize in Literature.

Acclaimed novelist Toni Morrison has used her poetic, magical prose to prove her contention that "if you study the culture and art of African Americans, you are not studying a regional or minor culture. What you are studying is America."

219. (True or False) A respected author of critical essays and a professor at Princeton, Toni Morrison became the first African American woman to have an endowed chair at an Ivy League college.

220. Before she became a successful full-time novelist, Toni Morrison was:

   a - *An advertising copywriter*
   b - *An editor who worked with many black authors*
   c - *A homemaker*

221. Elijah Muhammad traveled throughout the United States, spreading the teachings of what religious movement?

   a - *African Methodist Episcopal Church*
   b - *Black Muslims*
   c - *Black Jews*

222. What was Elijah Muhammad's given name?

   a - *Elijah Allen*
   b - *Elijah Poole*
   c - *Wallace Fard*

223. Elijah Muhammad and the Nation of Islam preached what for African Americans?

    a - *Political power*
    b - *Economic independence*
    c - *Racial integration*

224. (True or False) Elijah Muhammad was the founder of the Black Muslim movement.

225. Who replaced Elijah Muhammad in leading the Nation of Islam?

    a - *Louis Farrakhan*
    b - *Malcolm X*
    c - *Jesse Jackson*

226. (True or False) In 1950, the Associated Press named Jesse Owens the "greatest track-and-field athlete in history."

227. How many gold medals did Jesse Owens win at the 1936 Olympics?

    a - *2*
    b - *4*
    c - *5*

228. (True or False) At the conclusion of the 1936 Olympics, Jesse Owens was recognized as an "American hero" because he helped to discredit Nazi Germany's racist propaganda.

229. In the 1936 Olympics, what two events did Jesse Owens set new world records in?

    a - *100-meter dash and 400-meter relay*
    b - *Shot put and marathon*
    c - *200-meter dash and broad jump*

230. In addition to becoming a track star, Jesse Owens became the owner of three business ventures. What were they?

    a - *Football team; soccer team; restaurant owner*
    b - *Basketball team; dry cleaning company; public relations firm*
    c - *Real estate company; insurance company; clothing store*

231. (True or False) Satchel Paige was known throughout his career as the Man with a Thousand Windups.

232. Satchel Paige was the first African American to pitch in the major leagues. He played for what team?

  a - *New York Yankees*
  b - *Cleveland Indians*
  c - *Chicago White Sox*

233. In what year did Satchel Paige die?

  a - *1946*
  b - *1961*
  c - *1982*

234. At what age did Satchel Paige become a rookie in baseball's American League?

  a - *17*
  b - *33*
  c - *42*

235. How many lifetime victories did Satchel Paige have in his Negro leagues and major league career?

  a - *750*
  b - *1,207*
  c - *2,000*

236. Charlie Parker almost singlehandedly revolutionized the jazz world by perfecting the style known as:

  a - *Bebop*
  b - *Dixieland*
  c - *Blues*

237. What instrument did Charlie Parker play?

  a - *Clarinet*
  b - *Saxophone*
  c - *Piano*

238. Charlie Parker teamed up with what famous trumpeter?

  a - *Louis Armstrong*
  b - *Roy Eldridge*
  c - *Dizzy Gillespie*

239. What New York City nightclub was named after Charlie Parker?

    a - *Parker's*
    b - *Charlie's Lounge*
    c - *Birdland*

240. Before moving to the bustling jazz scene in New York, where did Charlie Parker refine his musical techniques?

    a - *New Orleans*
    b - *Kansas City*
    c - *Chicago*

241. What medium did Gordon Parks use to call attention to African American deprivation and racial discrimination?

    a - *Poetry*
    b - *Painting*
    c - *Photography*

242. What African American allowed Gordon Parks to publish a major story on the Black Muslim movement?

    a - *Elijah Muhammad*
    b - *Malcolm X*
    c - *Marcus Garvey*

243. Gordon Parks was voted "Magazine Photographer of the Year" in 1961 while working for what popular publication?

    a - *Time*
    b - *Newsweek*
    c - *Life*

244. Gordon Parks directed which famous movies?

    a - *Sounder* and *Cotton Comes to Harlem*
    b - *Old Yeller* and *The Cotton Club*
    c - *A Raisin in the Sun* and *To Sir with Love*

245. (True or False) Gordon Parks was the first African American to direct feature films for a major studio.

246. In which of the following movies did Sidney Poitier star?

    a - *To Sir with Love*
    b - *Six Degrees of Separation*
    c - *Trading Places*

247. *Guess Who's Coming to Dinner* was about:

    a - *An inner-city soup kitchen*
    b - *An interracial marriage*
    c - *A mystery solved by a southern black detective*

248. Sidney Poitier received his first Oscar nomination for Best Actor for what movie?

    a - *The Defiant Ones*
    b - *Lilies of the Field*
    c - *In the Heat of the Night*

249. Sidney Poitier was the first African American man to win the Academy Award for Best Actor. For what movie did he win?

    a - *The Blackboard Jungle*
    b - *Lilies of the Field*
    c - *Home of the Brave*

250. (True or False) A 1967 Gallup Poll found Sidney Poitier to be the most popular movie star in America.

251. What political office did Adam Clayton Powell, Jr., win in 1944?

    a - *Senator*
    b - *Congressman*
    c - *Mayor*

252. In New York City, Adam Clayton Powell, Jr., started out as a:

    a - *Lawyer*
    b - *Professor*
    c - *Minister*

253. What did the Powell amendment accomplish?

    a - *Voting rights for African Americans*
    b - *Denied federal money to any state that practiced segregation*
    c - *Awarded federal grants to African Americans pursuing higher education*

Before his retirement from the U.S. Army in 1993, Colin Powell became one of America's most prominent and influential military officials and an admired national hero, rising to the position of Chairman of the Joint Chiefs of Staff.

254. In the early 1960s, Adam Clayton Powell, Jr., embraced the militant views of what leader?

    a - *Martin Luther King, Jr.*
    b - *Malcolm X*
    c - *Ralph Abernathy*

255. Adam Clayton Powell, Jr., was chairman of what committee in the U.S. House of Representatives?

    a - *Ways and Means*
    b - *Environment*
    c - *Education and Labor*

256. What war led Colin Powell to conclude that an army should not enter into combat unless it had a clear objective?

    a - *Korean*
    b - *Vietnam*
    c - *World War II*

257. Colin Powell grew up in:

    a - *Baltimore*
    b - *Harlem*
    c - *The Bronx*

258. To what position was Colin Powell appointed, making him the highest ranking military officer— and the first African American and the youngest man to hold this post?

    a - *Four-star general*
    b - *Chairman of the Joint Chiefs of Staff*
    c - *National Security Adviser*

259. (True or False) In 1990, Colin Powell was responsible for directing Operation Desert Shield/Storm.

260. What U.S. president appointed Colin Powell National Security Adviser?

    a - *Gerald Ford*
    b - *Ronald Reagan*
    c - *George Bush*

261. (True or False) Asa Philip Randolph formed the American Federation of Labor in August 1925.

262. (True or False) Asa Philip Randolph was elected vice president of the AFL-CIO in 1957.

263. Before Asa Philip Randolph established a successful labor union for black train porters, approximately how much money were these workers paid per day?

    a - *$2.00*
    b - *$4.00*
    c - *$10.00*

264. Asa Philip Randolph's controversial, intellectual magazine was called:

    a - *The Crisis*
    b - *The Messenger*
    c - *The North Star*

265. In 1941, Asa Philip Randolph was the first to call for:

    a - *Black labor unions*
    b - *The desegregation of the U.S. armed forces*
    c - *A march on Washington*

266. (True or False) Paul Robeson played professional football to put himself through Columbia University Law School.

267. Paul Robeson's support of the Soviet Union was largely based on what quality he noticed in Russian people?

    a - *Lack of materialism*
    b - *Lack of racism*
    c - *Religious convictions*

268. What was the name of the Eugene O'Neill play that earned Paul Robeson critical praise?

    a - *Emperor Jones*
    b - *Showboat*
    c - *Les Miserables*

269. Paul Robeson was named "Champion of African Freedom" for his selfless service to Africa. He protested the jailing of what close friend?

    a - *Nelson Mandela*
    b - *Jomo Kenyatta*
    c - *Robert Mugabe*

270. What was the name of the Broadway play that starred Paul Robeson, making him the first black lead with a white supporting cast?

    a - *Macbeth*
    b - *Othello*
    c - *Raisin in the Sun*

271. Jackie Robinson began and ended his major league baseball career with what team?

    a - *The New York Yankees*
    b - *The Brooklyn Dodgers*
    c - *The Baltimore Orioles*

272. Jackie Robinson's primary position was:

    a - *Catcher*
    b - *First base*
    c - *Second base*

An intelligent, well-rounded actor and singer, Paul Robeson delivered powerful, nuanced performances onstage and worked devotedly offstage for human rights worldwide.

273. (True or False) In 1947, Jackie Robinson was given the Most Valuable Player Award.

274. Jackie Robinson played for what Negro leagues team?

> **a** - *Jersey City Giants*
> **b** - *Kansas City Monarchs*
> **c** - *New York Diamonds*

275. During his Hall of Fame career, Robinson:

> **a** - *Led the National League once in batting and twice in stolen bases*
> **b** - *Led his team to three World Series championships*
> **c** - *Led the National League once in batting and twice in home runs*

276. What disease did Wilma Rudolph have to overcome as a child?

    a - *Severe asthma*
    b - *Diabetes*
    c - *Polio*

277. In 1960, during the Rome Olympics, Wilma Rudolph became the fastest woman on earth. What was she called?

    a - *Road Runner*
    b - *Tennessee Tornado*
    c - *Golden Jet*

278. (True or False) The Wilma Rudolph Foundation was established to train and encourage tomorrow's sports stars.

279. At the 1960 Rome Olympics, in what events did Wilma Rudolph win her three gold medals?

    a - *100-meter dash; 200-meter dash; 400-meter dash*
    b - *100-meter dash; broad jump; shot put*
    c - *200-meter dash; 60-yard dash; 400-meter relay*

280. What was the name of Wilma Rudolph's relay team, which finished first at the 1960 Olympics?

    a - *Tennessee Tigerbelles*
    b - *Tennessee Roadsters*
    c - *Runnin' Relays*

281. Bill Russell became the nation's first African American head coach of what professional basketball team?

    a - *New York Knicks*
    b - *Philadelphia 76ers*
    c - *Boston Celtics*

282. Starting in 1959, Bill Russell led the Boston Celtics to how many straight NBA championships, an unprecedented accomplishment?

    a - *Four*
    b - *Six*
    c - *Eight*

283. How many times was Bill Russell voted the NBA's most valuable player?

  a - *Three*
  b - *Five*
  c - *Seven*

284. When Bill Russell failed to qualify for any of the sports teams in junior high school, he instead became a:

  a - *Team equipment manager*
  b - *Scorekeeper*
  c - *Team mascot (Indian Warrior)*

285. What baseball great played basketball with Bill Russell at McClymonds High School in Oakland, California?

  a - *Willie Stargell*
  b - *Frank Robinson*
  c - *Willie Mays*

286. (True or False) John Russwurm moved to Africa because he believed it was impossible for blacks to become American citizens.

287. Where was John Russwurm born?

  a - *Port Antonio, Jamaica*
  b - *Quebec, Canada*
  c - *Boston, Massachusetts*

288. John Russwurm was a pioneering journalist who pressed for:

  a - *The return of blacks to Africa*
  b - *Equal rights for blacks*
  c - *Black militant protest*

289. In 1836, John Russwurm was appointed governor of:

  a - *Maine*
  b - *The Liberia settlement*
  c - *Puerto Rico*

290. John Russwurm was the cofounder of America's first black newspaper. What was it called?

  a - *Freedom's Journal*
  b - *The Star*
  c - *The Negro Journal*

The first black player to break modern major league baseball's color barrier, Jackie Robinson not only compiled Hall of Fame–caliber statistics but also displayed inspiring personal dignity.

291. In 1850, what did Sojourner Truth have published?

    a - *The Narrative of Sojourner Truth*
    b - *Uncle Tom's Cabin*
    c - *Up from Slavery*

292. Although Sojourner Truth was illiterate, she became an outstanding:

    a - *Politician*
    b - *Public speaker*
    c - *Teacher*

293. Sojourner Truth passionately advocated:

    a - *Women's rights*
    b - *End of slavery*
    c - *Both a & b*

294. (True or False) Sojourner Truth worked as a spy during the Civil War.

295. What was Sojourner Truth's given name?

    a - *Isabella Baumfree*
    b - *Sally Hemmings*
    c - *Harriet Truth*

296. Harriet Tubman was affectionately called:

    a - *The best Underground Railroad conductor*
    b - *Aunt Harriet*
    c - *Moses*

297. (True or False) The U.S. government paid Harriet Tubman an $1,800.00 pension for her devoted military services during the Civil War.

298. How many trips did Harriet Tubman make to the South to rescue slaves?

    a - *8*
    b - *12*
    c - *19*

299. In 1863, what did the Union Army hire Harriet Tubman to do?

    a - *Spy on Confederates*
    b - *Nurse Union soldiers*
    c - *Both a & b*

300. Approximately how many slaves did Harriet Tubman lead to freedom?

    a - *200*
    b - *300*
    c - *500*

301. When was Denmark Vesey's black army organized to fight slavery?

    a - *Ten years after the Civil War*
    b - *Forty years before the Civil War*
    c - *Five years after the Revolutionary War*

302. What happened to Denmark Vesey after he was convicted of raising an insurrection against slave owners?

    a - *He was sold back into slavery*
    b - *He was hanged*
    c - *He was deported to Africa*

303. Where did Denmark Vesey plan to launch an attack in an effort to release blacks from bondage?

    a - *Charleston, South Carolina*
    b - *Savannah, Georgia*
    c - *Charlotte, North Carolina*

304. How did Denmark Vesey gain his freedom?

    a - *Won money in a lottery and purchased his freedom*
    b - *Fled north into Canada*
    c - *Slave owner gave him his freedom*

305. Denmark Vesey settled in South Carolina, a state that suspended the slave trade in 1787. In 1803, what agricultural boom made the slave trade popular again?

    a - *Cotton boom*
    b - *Tobacco boom*
    c - *Wheat and corn boom*

306. Who played the role of Celie in the movie version of Alice Walker's best-selling book *The Color Purple*?

    a - *Oprah Winfrey*
    b - *Whoopi Goldberg*
    c - *Cicely Tyson*

307. Alice Walker advised what movie director during the film production of *The Color Purple*?

    a - *Spike Lee*
    b - *John Singleton*
    c - *Steven Spielberg*

308. Alice Walker's *Meridian* is a novel about what?

    a - *Slavery*
    b - *Civil rights movement*
    c - *African culture*

309. What Alice Walker novel dealt with the controversial topic of African female genital mutilation?

    a - *The Third Life of Grange Copeland*
    b - *The Temple of My Familiar*
    c - *Possessing the Secret of Joy*

310. (True or False) Alice Walker won the Pulitzer Prize for *The Temple of My Familiar.*

311. What did Madam C. J. Walker invent in 1905 that was sold door-to-door?

    a - *Hair care preparation for blacks*
    b - *Perfume*
    c - *Brushes*

312. (True or False) Madam C. J. Walker is considered to be the first African American female millionaire.

313. What image did Madam C. J. Walker use on her product's packages?

    a - *Harriet Tubman*
    b - *Her own likeness*
    c - *High fashion models*

314. What was Madam C. J. Walker's occupation prior to starting her own business?

    a - *Housekeeper*
    b - *Washerwoman*
    c - *Beautician*

315. In 1905, Madam C. J. Walker invented and received a patent for the:

    a - *Hairbrush*
    b - *Hair dryer*
    c - *Hair-straightening comb*

316. (True or False) In 1856, Booker T. Washington was born a free man.

317. (True or False) Booker T. Washington advised presidents Grover Cleveland, William McKinley, and Theodore Roosevelt.

318. Booker T. Washington was the founder and president of what educational institution?

    a - *Meharry Medical College*
    b - *Howard University*
    c - *Tuskegee Institute*

319. In what famous speech did Booker T. Washington ask blacks to postpone their demands for equal rights and focus on improving themselves through education?

    a - *"Free at Last"*
    b - *"Atlanta Compromise"*
    c - *"March on Washington"*

320. (True or False) Booker T. Washington first hired scientist Lewis Latimer and fostered his research career.

321. Richard Wright's first novel, *Native Son,* described:

    a - *Life as a slave*
    b - *Black ghetto life*
    c - *African lifestyles*

322. In 1945, Richard Wright published his autobiography entitled:

    a - *Black Boy*
    b - *Native Son*
    c - *Uncle Tom's Children*

323. Richard Wright wrote a searing collection of stories entitled:

    a - *Uncle Tom's Cabin*
    b - *Uncle Tom's Children*
    c - *The Weary Blues*

324. What was the name of the fictional character in Richard Wright's book *Native Son*?

    a - *Janie Crawford*
    b - *Jess B. Semple*
    c - *Bigger Thomas*

325. Which of the following books were written by Richard Wright?

    a - *Black Power; Black Boy; White Man Listen*
    b - *The Conjure Woman; The House Behind the Cedars; The Colonel's Dream*
    c - *I, Too, Sing America; Invisible Man; The Color Purple*

ANSWERS

1. a **Milwaukee Braves**
2. a **755**
3. a **Hammerin' Hank**
4. c **1956**
5. **False - The Milwaukee Braves**
6. b **Joe Frazier**
7. a **Drew "Bundini" Brown**
8. a **George Foreman**
9. **True**
10. b **Threw it in the Ohio River to protest America's racism**
11. **True**
12. c **African Methodist Episcopal Church**
13. a **American Society of Free Persons of Colour**
14. c **The church had a discriminatory seating policy**
15. **True**
16. a **Philadelphia**
17. a **"Voice of the American Soul"**
18. **False - She was the first black singer**
19. a **U.S. delegate to the United Nations**
20. b **Eleanor Roosevelt publicly announced her resignation from the DAR**
21. c **New Orleans**
22. c **"Hello Dolly"**
23. a **Satchmo**
24. a **Jazz**
25. b **King Oliver's Creole Jazz Band**
26. b **Ranked number one in men's tennis**
27. c **Jimmy Connors**
28. c **Heart attack**
29. c **U.S. Open**
30. a **Sportsman of the Year**
31. b **The Charleston**
32. a **Benefit performance for the civil rights movement**
33. a **French Military Intelligence**
34. b **Rosette of the Resistance/Legion of Honor**
35. a **Folies-Bergère**
36. a **A young minister in Harlem**
37. b **Racial understanding**
38. c **Robert F. Kennedy**

39. a *Notes of a Native Son; The Fire Next Time*
40. True
41. True
42. b Almanac
43. c Washington, D.C.
44. b The first wooden clock in the American colonies
45. a Thomas Jefferson
46. a LeRoi Jones
47. b *Blues People*
48. b Plays
49. c Congress of Afrikan Peoples
50. a Harlem (New York City)
51. True
52. a "One O'Clock Jump"
53. c Billie Holiday
54. c "Fly Me to the Moon"
55. b "I Can't Stop Loving You"
56. True
57. a Social worker
58. b National Medal of Arts
59. b A distinguished art historian
60. True
61. c Beckwourth Pass
62. True
63. b Sierra Nevada
64. b Pueblo, Colorado
65. a The Crow
66. b Booker T. Washington
67. a Bethune-Cookman College
68. a Black Cabinet
69. b National Council of Negro Women
70. a Division of Negro Affairs, National Youth Administration
71. b Race relations
72. True
73. c Both a & b
74. c Africa
75. b Mediating the Arab-Israeli conflict
76. True
77. c 325
78. b Thomas Edison
79. b 1864
80. c Booker T. Washington
81. b Black novelist
82. b $10.00
83. a *The House Behind the Cedars*
84. b The fate of mixed-bloods in a racist society
85. True
86. c Philadelphia
87. True

88. a **Dr. Cliff Huxtable**
89. a *Fatherhood*
90. b **"I Spy"**
91. **False - In Africa**
92. a **Shipbuilding and shipping**
93. c **Sierra Leone**
94. a **Marcus Garvey**
95. b **Refused to pay taxes**
96. b **Haiti**
97. a *The North Star*
98. c **Abraham Lincoln**
99. **True**
100. c **Fifteenth Amendment**
101. c **Blood bank program**
102. c **American Red Cross**
103. b **Doctor of Science in Medicine**
104. b **Howard University**
105. **True**
106. **True**
107. a **National Association for the Advancement of Colored People**
108. a *The Crisis*
109. b **Harvard**
110. b **Ghana**
111. b **12**
112. **True**
113. **True**
114. a *Lyrics of Lowly Life*
115. c **Orville and Wilbur Wright**
116. a **African and Caribbean**
117. b **Albert Schweitzer Music Award**
118. b **Anthropologist**
119. a **Metropolitan Opera House**
120. b *Tropics and Le Jazz Hot: From Haiti to Harlem*
121. b **Jazz**
122. b **The Cotton Club**
123. a **Edward Kennedy Ellington**
124. c **2,000**
125. b **"Take the 'A' Train"**
126. c **Music**
127. b **Richard Wright**
128. a *Invisible Man*
129. **False**
130. a **How deeply American culture has been influenced by the black experience**
131. **True**
132. b **Congress of Racial Equality**
133. c **Sit-in Movement; Freedom Rides**
134. a **Shirley Chisholm**
135. b **To integrate interstate travel and bus stations**

136. c "First Lady of Song"
137. a Memorex
138. b "Love You Madly"
139. a "A Tisket, a Tasket"
140. c Chick Webb Orchestra
141. b Back to Africa Movement
142. a Black Moses
143. c Universal Negro Improvement Association
144. b Black Star Line
145. b Booker T. Washington
146.   True
147. b French Championship
148.   False - To sharecropper parents
149. b 1957, 1958
150. a Golf
151.   True
152. c Inuit
153. a 1909
154. b 18
155. c Nicaragua
156. b *Cotton Comes to Harlem*
157. b Prison
158. a Marcus Garvey
159.   True
160. c *The Quality of Hurt*
161. a Jazz singers
162. a *Lady Sings the Blues*
163. a Drug abuse
164. b Count Basie
165. b "Strange Fruit"
166. b The poet laureate of Harlem
167.   True
168. c "Ode to Freedom"
169. b Jazz and blues
170. c Jess B. Semple
171. b *Their Eyes Were Watching God*
172. c To gather folklore
173. a Voodoo rituals in the Caribbean
174. b Harlem Renaissance
175.   False - Alice Walker
176. b Operation PUSH
177. a Martin Luther King, Jr.
178. c Walter Mondale and Michael Dukakis
179.   True
180. b "Keep hope alive."
181. c Sermon poetry
182. b National Association for the Advancement of Colored People
183. b *The Autobiography of an Ex-Colored Man*
184. b "Lift Every Voice and Sing"

185.   **True**
186. c **Piano**
187. b **Ragtime**
188. a **One cent**
189. a **A Pulitzer Prize**
190. b **"The Entertainer"**
191.   **True**
192. b **Congresswoman**
193. b **Become a lawyer**
194. b **Jimmy Carter**
195. a **Calling for the impeachment of Richard Nixon**
196.   **False - He was the youngest**
197. b **The Montgomery bus boycott**
198. b **Southern Christian Leadership Conference**
199. c **The Lincoln Memorial**
200. c **Both a & b**
201. c **Militant action**
202. a **Nation of Islam**
203. b **Alex Haley**
204. c **1965**
205.   **True**
206. b **Mr. Civil Rights**
207. a ***Brown v. Board of Education of Topeka***
208. c **Lyndon B. Johnson**
209.   **True**
210. a **Determined that the "Separate but Equal" doctrine has no place in education**
211. c ***Challenger***
212.   **False - Guion Bluford, Jr.**
213. c **Mission science specialist**
214.   **False - MIT**
215.   **True**
216. b ***The Bluest Eye***
217. c ***Beloved***
218.   **True**
219.   **True**
220. b **An editor who worked with many black authors**
221. b **Black Muslims**
222. b **Elijah Poole**
223. b **Economic independence**
224.   **False - W. D. Fard**
225. a **Louis Farrakhan**
226.   **True**
227. b **4**
228.   **True**
229. c **200-meter dash and broad jump**
230. b **Basketball team; dry cleaning company; public relations firm**
231.   **True**
232. b **Cleveland Indians**

233. c **1982**
234. c **42**
235. c **2,000**
236. a **Bebop**
237. b **Saxophone**
238. c **Dizzy Gillespie**
239. c **Birdland**
240. b **Kansas City**
241. c **Photography**
242. b **Malcolm X**
243. c *Life*
244. a *Sounder* and *Cotton Comes to Harlem*
245.   **True**
246. a *To Sir with Love*
247. b **An interracial marriage**
248. a *The Defiant Ones*
249. b *Lilies of the Field*
250.   **True**
251. b **Congressman**
252. c **Minister**
253. b **Denied federal money to any state that practiced segregation**
254. b **Malcolm X**
255. c **Education and Labor**
256. b **Vietnam**
257. c **The Bronx**
258. b **Chairman of the Joint Chiefs of Staff**
259.   **True**
260. b **Ronald Reagan**
261.   **False - The Brotherhood of Sleeping Car Porters**
262.   **True**
263. a **$ 2.00**
264. b *The Messenger*
265. c **A march on Washington**
266.   **True**
267. b **Lack of racism**
268. a *Emperor Jones*
269. b **Jomo Kenyatta**
270. b *Othello*
271. b **Brooklyn Dodgers**
272. c **Second base**
273.   **False - The Rookie of the Year Award**
274. b **Kansas City Monarchs**
275. a **Led the National League once in batting and twice in stolen bases**
276. c **Polio**
277. b **Tennessee Tornado**
278.   **True**
279. a **100-meter dash; 200-meter dash; 400-meter dash**

280. a **Tennessee Tigerbelles**
281. c **Boston Celtics**
282. c **Eight**
283. b **Five**
284. c **Team mascot (Indian Warrior)**
285. b **Frank Robinson**
286.   **True**
287. a **Port Antonio, Jamaica**
288. b **Equal rights for blacks**
289. b **The Liberia settlement**
290. a *Freedom's Journal*
291. a *The Narrative of Sojourner Truth*
292. b **Public speaker**
293. c **Both a & b**
294.   **False - An administrator in Freedmen's Hospital**
295. a **Isabella Baumfree**
296. c **Moses**
297.   **False - She received no pension and was left penniless by the U.S. government due to the color of her skin.**
298. c **19**
299. c **Both a & b**
300. b **300**
301. b **Forty years before the Civil War**
302. b **He was hanged**
303. a **Charleston, South Carolina**
304. a **Won money in a lottery and purchased his freedom**
305. a **Cotton boom**
306. b **Whoopi Goldberg**
307. c **Steven Spielberg**
308. b **Civil rights movement**
309. c *Possessing the Secret of Joy*
310.   **False - *The Color Purple***
311. a **Hair care preparation for blacks**
312.   **True**
313. b **Her own likeness**
314. b **Washerwoman**
315. c **Hair-straightening comb**
316.   **False - He was born into slavery**
317.   **True**
318. c **Tuskegee Institute**
319. b **"Atlanta Compromise"**
320.   **False - George Washington Carver**
321. b **Black ghetto life**
322. a *Black Boy*
323. b *Uncle Tom's Children*
324. c **Bigger Thomas**
325. a *Black Power; Black Boy; White Man Listen*

INDEX

R.S. RENNERT has edited the nearly 100 volumes in Chelsea House's award-winning BLACK AMERICANS OF ACHIEVEMENT series, which tells the stories of black men and women who have helped shape the course of modern history, and the 10 volumes in the PROFILES OF GREAT BLACK AMERICANS series. He is also the author of several sports biographies, including *Henry Aaron, Jesse Owens,* and *Jackie Robinson.*